Inspirational Memories

WRITTEN BY: G. ALBERT BROWN, JR.

*This book is dedicated
to all my friends,
past and present,
with love.*

TABLE OF CONTENTS

INTRODUCTION

When I first began reading and organizing the materials collected herein, I found two lines in a poem entitled, Beyond The Grave, that seemed to capture the character of the author more than any words I could write.

The words read,

"Teaching others with my prayerful talk
And matching it daily with my faithful walk."

Anyone who knows Dr. G. Albert Brown, Jr. would have to agree.

Dr. Brown is the pastor of the Crossroads Baptist Church in Fredericksburg, Virginia. He is Founder and President of the Fredericksburg Bible Institute.

He is an active evangelist and it was in a revival where I first met him.

He was in the middle of several weeks of back to back revivals and the grueling schedule had begun to show. However, when he took his position in the pulpit, the faith and conviction that forces this man on, took hold and the tired, quiet man grew into a full force gospel storm.

He carries his profound beliefs and trust into each new endeavor with zest and total commitment.

It is with the same emotion and the innermost desire to serve and praise the Lord that he now chooses to share these inspirational thoughts, ideas and memories.

May this book be as much a blessing to everyone who reads it, as the author is to those who know him.

— Donna Lee Schwertfeger
February 1989

Memories

BEYOND THE GRAVE

When I close my eyes for sleep
I know my soul is in the Master's keep.
Not knowing where I will awake,
But whether here or there, it's for the Lord's sake.

Having put my Faith in Him to save,
Being assured there is life beyond the grave.
Jesus died that I might live
That in this life I am willing to give.

I was dedicated to my church
With notes in my Bible and pages to search;
Teaching others with my prayerful talk
And matching it daily with my faithful walk.

I have experienced much suffering and pain
But when it is all over, there will be Heaven to gain;
Because Jesus who came from Heaven above
Has made my reservations by His love.

Leaving behind my daughters and son,
Knowing that with them the battle is won,
Because where I'm going there is no sorrow
Looking to see my family and friends on that great tomorrow.

BORN TO DIE

In Memory of My Invalid Sister

Faye Ellen was referred to as a little girl
Having shared over 40 years in this world.
Being an invalid, it was very hard to live
With no contribution of service to ever give.

Great love was shown by her father and mother
And a great devotion by the wife of her brother.
In this life she never learned to talk
Nor did her condition permit her to walk.

Today she is walking on the streets of gold
Because the old rugged cross atoned for her soul.
We know all things work together for our best,
A long time of suffering was exchanged for rest.

She spent her life as a patient in bed
Then one day the announcement came — she is dead.
But hello in heaven, is a down here goodbye
Knowing her purpose in life was Born to Die.

A TRUE FRIEND

In Memory of Murray Bland Seward,
My Employer for Eight Years

When the call came I was in bed,
To receive the news that Seward was dead.
At first my impulse was very sad;
Knowing he was a Christian, I was also glad.

He has suffered a long time in this life,
But standing by his side was a devoted wife.
Absent from the body is to be present with God,
Even though his body will be placed beneath the sod.

We shared times of happiness, frustration, and tears;
Having worked for him for a period of eight years;
To discover he has always been a true friend.
To know him was to trust him even to the end.

He has experienced much family tragedy and pain,
But as a child of God, we know it is Heaven's gain,
As a Christian, his witness on earth was great,
Knowing one day he too, would enter the pearly gates.

Now that he is in Heaven waiting to greet
All the saved who are waiting the Savior to meet;
Trusting that none would ever be lost,
Knowing that salvation was purchased at the cross.

LIFE WITH JESUS

In Memory of Ethel Sanders

She was a very devoted wife
Which was demonstrated by her life
Expressing her love for one another
While proving to be a great mother.

Her children knew her personal care
With all the concern parents share
Knowing with confidence God would provide
Keeping the family together by His side.

Life is filled with heartaches and sorrows
But each day we hope for a brighter tomorrow
Realizing that all answers are in God's Son
And by faith in Him all battles will be won.

Awaiting to see that great day
When my family and friends are on the way
To be greeted by her with a loving smile
Saying life with Jesus is worthwhile.

WITHOUT HIS LOVE

In Memory of Floyd Sanders

When I awoke to begin the day
I thought everything was well,
Until I heard a voice from Heaven say,
Your guardian angel is ringing the bell.

The toll of the bell kept on ringing
As death came to set me free.
I could hear the Heavenly chorus singing,
This is the way God wants it to be.

Early in the morning I surrendered to death
Because I knew my time had come;
As I prepared to breathe my last breath
I knew in Christ the battle was won.

I suffered for many years in this life,
But to know in Heaven there is no pain.
My favorite nurse has been my wife
And eternal rest is mine to gain.

When it is time to change our dwelling place
And our attention is focused above;
We must look in the Master's face
To know there is nothing to life without His love.

FOR CHRIST, HIS BEST

In Memory of Frank Voight

Frank Voight was a great man,
Dedicating his life to God's plan.
Here today and gone tomorrow,
Bringing to many sudden sorrow.

He has walked his last earthly mile,
Being remembered always for his smile.
For anyone who had a need or care
He was willing to help and share.

To be in his presence was a pleasure
With an expression of love as his treasure.
We know not the day or the hour
That death will claim us by God's power.

Where he has gone, there is no night,
For Christ is the source of everlasting light.
He is now abiding in his eternal rest,
Leaving as a testimony, for Christ, his best.

GOODBYE FOR A LITTLE WHILE

In Memory of Rosalie Boyle

She was a loving and devoted wife
With the attributes of a Christian life.
To her children, an understanding mother
Realized by them, there was no other.

Her face had a radiant glow
Which was genuine and not a show.
From within the heart was that love
That she had received from God above.

Her Bible, to her, was the greatest book,
Receiving a new revelation with every look.
She read her Bible throughout the years
Many times wetting the pages with her tears.

Her suffering at times was hard to bear,
Drawing on the strength that Christ would share.
Making each day of sickness a pleasure
With the cross being her God given treasure.

She was not afraid to die,
Because in Christ, she could say goodbye.
Just gone away for a little while
Waiting to greet her family and friends with a smile.

(This poem was also read at the funeral of Mrs. Hilda Cates.)

TO SAY GOODBYE

In Memory of Leola O. Dietz

I only knew her for a little while,
But through it all she wore a smile.
She was a dedicated and devoted mother.
To take her place there is no other.

She spent much of her time in the home,
Which she has left, no more to roam.
Her present residence is now in Heaven
Because of the salvation that is God given.

She lived to reach a good old age.
Her life was filled with love on every page.
Being confident she had done her best,
Then the Lord said enter eternal rest.

Having been a Christian all these years,
Let our Christ wipe away your tears.
As she waits for her family in the sky,
Having departed only to say goodbye.

WILLING TO HELP

In Memory of George Weimer

He was not just a man
Who enjoyed working with his hands;
But he was vigorous and strong,
Willing to work all day long.

I remember him for his humor and smile,
Realizing we are only separated for a while.
It brought joy to have him as a friend,
And being assured that death is not the end.

He was devoted to his children and wife,
Sharing a Christian testimony all of his life.
To everyone he was considerate and kind,
Willing to help anyone at anytime.

Knowing now he has entered into perfect rest,
Which is life at its best;
Where there is no suffering, pain, or sorrow.
All who know Jesus will see him tomorrow.

PROMOTION DAY

**In Memory of George Williams,
First Deacon Chairman of Crossroads Baptist Church
and a very dear friend in the faith.**

George Williams is the person's name
In which the Death Angel made his claim;
Only to remove him from suffering and pain
And to reassure the family of Heaven's gain.

We can hear the Spirit's still, small voice say,
This is George William' Promotion Day.
Having been to many a dear, loving friend
And convinced that death is not the end.

He leaves a testimony of a dedicated life.
Standing by his side was a devoted wife.
His love as a father was shared with his sons.
His eternal life with his Heavenly Father was won.

He was a master in the upholstery trade.
Every job resulted in friends that he made;
Believing that no handicap would hinder his soul
And one day he would walk the streets of gold.

MOMMA HALL

In Memory of Dr. Bill Hall's Mother

She listened attentively for God's call
To hear the death angel say, Momma Hall,
Come with me to your Heavenly place
Prepared by God's gift of loving grace.

You know on earth you have done your best
And now the time has come for eternal rest.
While your body is to be placed under the sod
Your soul will be forever in the presence of God.

Her hair was as white as snow.
Her smile had had a heavenly glow.
Her life here was eighty-two years
Knowing God would wipe away all her tears.

Her suffering at last was constant pain,
But her faith would never let her complain.
For her family she expressed great care
With a guiding hand for the life up there.

SUNSHINE

In Memory of Mrs. Annie Harris
(Sunshine was her nickname for Dr. Brown.
She said he brought sunshine into her life.)

God is the one who gives us breath;
He also takes it with the act of death.
But for those over one hundred years,
We accept it with joy and not tears.

Her life was lived with Heaven as a goal.
Being born again with salvation of the soul.
The last years of her life were a real test
But through her suffering she did her best.

With Scriptures that were hidden in her heart
She touched many people with love as she taught.
For this precious one the sun has set in the west,
After years of sickness, now there is sweet rest.

Even though for many years there was no sight,
She said, God's purpose for this is right.
For a saint to die, we do not express sorrow
Because we know we will see her tomorrow.

GOD KNOWS BEST

In Memory of Chris Carter

Chris was a brilliant child,
Wrapping his life in a smile.
Never known to ever complain
With his suffering of daily pain.

He spent most of his life in bed,
Listening to every word the doctor said.
Believing Jesus to be Doctor in Chief,
Accepting major surgery with little grief.

He was young in experience and years
But mature in controlling his tears;
To help his parents understand
That he was a brave young man.

He heard God's voice say, "You are mine.
I am sending my angel for you at the age of nine
To relieve your suffering in eternal rest,
Wanting you to know my decision is best."

NO LONGER BLIND

In Memory of Mrs. Louise Wright

She has moved to a new home,
Never again to ever roam.
It is located in the sky
And to enter she had to die.

In Jesus there is victory over death,
Available to anyone with breath;
Focusing attention to the cross,
Accepting Him will never be lost.

For thirty years there was no sight,
Daily strengthened with His love and might.
Knowing one day she would again see
When her Master said, "Come with me."

This is earth's loss and Heaven's gain,
Released from all her suffering and pain.
Thanking everyone who has been so kind,
Thankful to God that she's no longer blind.

SHE SAYS GOODBYE

In Memory of Elva S. Balderson

Even though she lived above seventy years
To give her up brings sorrow and tears.
She was known in life as a friend and mother
Who expressed her friendship like no other.

Whenever you saw her she had a smile,
Even if your visit was for a little while.
Through her suffering, sickness, and pain
She was always confident Heaven was to gain.

She loved her children and this they knew,
So they provided for her faithful and true.
She had two daughters and one son
A close family where the needs were none.

For life down here, she says goodbye,
To move into her mansion in the sky,
And with the ones gone on before her she waits
To greet others at the pearly gates.

EVERYTHING IS ALL RIGHT
In Memory of Carl Brooks

I want to go to my Heavenly home
And end my journey on earth to roam.
I can hear the sound of bells ringing
And I know the angels above are singing.

To Jesus Christ I have given my life,
Having been loved and encouraged by my wife.
The last years of my life have given much pain
But now being released with Heaven to gain.

Through my faith with God given power
I was able to withstand the darkest hour,
Because through Christ, my Savior, there is light,
Assurance of the new birth, everything is all right.

Thank you family and friends for being so kind
And all the wonderful memories that have been mine,
Now receiving my robe of righteousness to wear,
Saying to all, goodbye here and hello there.

SHARED HIS LIFE

In Memory of John W. Seay

He was an appreciated and respected man,
One who lived his life with a daily plan.
Searching for answers and the reason why,
Ready for whatever happened, even to die.

He loved his children and devoted wife.
For them he dedicated and shared his life.
While he was healthy and physically strong,
He worked and labored, never seeking wrong.

Over two decades I have known him as a friend,
One who could be trusted, even to the end.
Now that God through death has sent release
He is resting with Christ, in perfect peace.

GREET YOU IN HEAVEN

In Memory of Anna Green

Down here she was Anna Green.
Up there she is a Heavenly being.
Down here she was known and loved by all.
Up there she is one redeemed from the fall.

Wanting to go was her goal.
Now she has arrived both in spirit and soul.
The day she breathed her last breath
The door of Heaven was opened by death.

She was one who could laugh and smile
And always willing to go the second mile.
With a life that was dedicated to the end
To the many who knew her, always a friend.

She loved her family and her church,
Pointing others upward in their search;
Knowing one day she would say goodbye
And wait to greet you in Heaven on High.

A nchored in faith in Christ
N eighbor to all who knew her
N ame in the Lamb's book of Life
A nswered the Heavenly call peacefully

ROBE OF WHITE

In Memory of Elsie Sanders

I want to remember her in the robe of white,
By this I know everything is all right.
This robe is because of Christ and His love
Which came to all believers from above.

Her life was more than a wife and mother
As she spent much of it helping others.
In her quiet, willing, and humble way
She expressed her interest in service everyday.

With years of dedication as a devoted wife,
Rearing her children and sharing her life;
Everything she attempted was given her best.
One day she knew that work would stop for eternal rest.

This robe of white is more than a nurse's gown,
It's His righteousness for us who are Heavenly bound;
Knowing that He gave His all at Calvary
So God's salvation is for you and me.

Check to see if you have the robe of grace
And that your name is reserved for a Heavenly place;
And when death has knocked and turned off the light
The only hope we have is that robe of White.

LIFE WILL NEVER END

In Memory of David Cardwell Thomas

When God chooses to give eternal rest
He wants us to know what happens is best.
Having lived threescore and ten years,
It still brings heartache and many tears.

Now that he is no longer in pain,
Suffering is gone, but Heaven to gain;
Having this as his ultimate goal,
Being assured it is well with his soul.

One who was not afraid of death
And was conscious af his last breath;
We ask the age old question why,
Does a person live and also have to die?

Our visits were only for a short while,
But he always greeted us with a smile.
Being dedicated to his family and friends
To live with Christ, life will never end.

GREET YOU TOMORROW

In Memory of Mrs. Hazel Headley

When we turn the pages of her life,
The records reveal a good mother and devoted wife.
Having set Heaven as her ultimate goal
Because Jesus had saved her soul.

She was dedicated and loyal to her church
With a Bible full of notes and references to search.
Always willing whenever asked to teach,
That her talents would help in others to reach.

She loved her daughters and her son
Knowing with them the battle was won.
She would close her eyes in eternal sleep
Being assured that their souls were in the Master's keep.

She worked hard among her friends,
Never thinking about the day's end.
Her earthly labors now have ceased
Because the Master has sent for her release.

This testimony speaks to all who are saved
To hear the Master say there is life beyond the grave.
Having suffered here with pain and sorrow
But waiting to greet you on that tomorrow.

RESTING WITH CHRIST

In Memory of George Cooley

He was a quiet, reserved man
Who lived his life with a plan.
Knowing what he believed and why,
Ready for the end, even to die.

He loved his children and his wife.
For them he sacrificed his life.
As long as he was physically strong
He worked and labored, seeking no wrong.

The years I have known him, he was a friend.
Through work or sickness, even to the end.
Now that God through death has sent release,
He is resting with Christ in perfect peace.

NO TEARS

In Memory of Mason Gray

Death knocked one day
And called Mason Gray,
Come and with Me abide
Said God from the other side.

This life has been long
But as beautiful as a song,
With trials of every day
Turned to joy along the way.

Each day I did my best
Knowing someday I would rest,
To find peace with the Almighty God
Before placing my body in the sod.

So the witness I leave behind
Is to let your light shine
To others who will walk
In the path of your talk.

Live each day with a smile
Counting the steps in every mile.
Being reminded of the many years
That only God can wipe away tears.

ABIDE WITH ME

In Memory of Elmer Wesley Elliott

He departed peacefully from this life,
While standing by his side was his wife.
His sister and his minister were also by his bed
When they heard the final words the doctor said.

His suffering was truly a tremendous fight,
But the decision now is that which is right.
Because of his faith he kept looking above,
Having in his heart the Christ of love.

He loved his family, friends, and church
Allowing the Lord to make a daily search.
That his testimony before others would bring
A satisfied heart and a song to sing.

To many of his friends he was "Captain Wes"
But unto the Lord he had stood the test.
Because one day on the Heavenly C.B.
He heard the Master say, Come abide with me.

HER SMILE

In Memory of Doris L. Flagg

S aved — by faith in Jesus.
M other — appreciated by her children.
I ntegrity — trustworthy and respected.
L oved — by everyone who knew her.
E ntrance — into eternal glory.

She was known by her smile,
Loved and appreciated by every child.
When the news came about her death
We could not believe it was her last breath.

But God who never makes a mistake,
Was ready for her soul to take.
Now having entered into eternal rest,
She has been able to stand the test.

Having had her for sixty-two years
We must let her memory wipe away the tears.
Even though it has brought us sorrow
We plan now to see her tomorrow.

Lived here as a good mother and dedicated wife,
Now reunited with her husband in eternal life.
Always remembering our family tie,
Departing now is just a short goodbye.

HER ETERNAL HOME

In Memory of Margaret Kirk Coakley

Mother has entered her eternal home,
Never again in this sinful world to roam.
Not knowing when it would take place,
But convinced it happened by God's grace.

Having shared this life for many years,
Experiencing its heartaches, suffering, and tears,
Being assured these one day would pass
And complete happiness would dominate at last.

While in this world she did her best,
Long hours of work with very little rest.
Knowing she must stand before Him one day
To receive for her labors an honest pay.

But now that she is separated and over there,
She can talk to Jesus face to face, not in prayer.
Drawing on His love like never before,
Realizing once and for all He is Heaven's Door.

Standing with Him and waiting to greet
All in Christ who claim their eternal seat.
Because of her absence you are now in sorrow
But you shall see her one bright tomorrow.

Until then, live and love
With your heart focused above.
Knowing the security of your soul...
It is your earthly blessing and your Heavenly goal.

A FRIEND TO THE END

In Memory of Lewis Durrette
Chairman of the Pulpit Committee when I
Came as Pastor to Spotswood.

When the news came announcing his death,
His healing also came with his last breath.
He had struggled a long time to gain life
And standing by his side was his devoted wife.

He was dedicated and committed to his church
Encouraging others as a part of his daily search.
Telling them of Jesus and His Divine love,
Helping to prepare people for their home above.

He was a man who always did his best
Willing to sacrifice and stand the test.
He was a family man and worked hard too,
Providing for his own as best he knew.

His desire was to die at home,
To depart this life and in Heaven to roam;
Knowing his illness would not mend,
But to everyone, he was a friend to the end.

A GOOD MAN

In Memory of Wallace Robinson

Wallace Robinson was a good man
And that was not hard to understand
He lived a quiet dedicated life
Sharing every day with his son and wife.

His passing has brought about tears
Having to give him up after many years
But we know it is well with his soul
Because to be in Heaven was his goal.

He had many neighbors and friends
They knew him to be trustworthy to the end
His witness for Christ was to be kind
And to let his daily light shine.

Now that his soul is at rest
And he having given his best
Is now awaiting in Heaven to see
All his loved ones — you and me.

FAITH IN CHRIST

In Memory of Mrs. June Nestor

She closed her eyes as if to sleep,
Placing her soul in the Master's keep.
Never again to know sickness or sorrow
But the happiness of that great tomorrow.

Her life was an expression of love,
Looking to Jesus to return from above;
Being a true witness to every race
With countenance reflecting Jesus' face.

Her message was, it will be all right,
Because where I am going there is no night.
Our time together has been many years,
So let our love wipe away all tears.

When the recording angel opens the book
And through its pages takes a look,
The name of June Nestor will be found
Because her faith in Christ was sound.

HIS FOUR "H" LIFE

In Memory of John Wesley Walsh

With his **HANDS** he enjoyed his work
Never an opportunity would he ever shirk.

Within his **HEART** love always lived
And of this love to others he would give.

The doors of his **HOME** were open all the time
And upon every knock the welcome was kind.

His **HOPE** finally resulted in eternal rest
Leaving this life, having done his best.

ALWAYS A FRIEND

In Memory of Irma Oliff

She was a person gracious, sweet, and kind
Having lived this life sixty years and nine.
Always willing to do someone a good deed,
Helping everyone regardless of the need.

Once she knew you, then always a friend,
The same person to everyone until the end.
Her life was a demonstration of true love,
Her faith in Christ was her passport above.

Realizing that God knows for us what is best
When He is ready for us to enter eternal rest;
Where there will be no sickness or pain,
But comfort, happiness, and Heaven to gain.

Knowing one day she would breathe her last breath,
The Pearly Gates would open by the angel of death;
Requesting that her family no longer be in sorrow
Because she would be waiting for them tomorrow.

THE PRIME OF LIFE

In Memory of Marty Price

It was a shock about the news of his death
When we realized there was no breath.
Was then we asked the unanswerable question why
Did in the prime of his life, did he have to die?

We will remember him by his smile;
Knowing he will be separated for a while;
Then together again we will be
As we gather one day across the sea.

Until then we will patiently wait,
When the knob will turn on Heaven's gate
And hear the angel's beckoning cry,
Come on in here, where there is no goodbye.

HIS GREATEST JOY

**In Memory of Wilbur Wallace,
Trustee of Crossroads Baptist Church**

Wilbur Wallace was a man of integrity,
Because of his believing faith in Calvary.
I stood beside his bed the last day of his life
With one hand in mine and the other in his wife's.

He was a man who had many close friends
And lived what he believed until the end.
Ready to go, he obeyed God's voice,
Knowing in Christ this was his eternal choice.

Now that he has entered into perfect rest,
He has suffered long, but stood the test.
He served his country and county well,
His greatest joy, the love of Christ to tell.

Having lived in this world almost fourscore years
We are saddened with an expression of tears.
Let's dwell on the years we had him to love
And get ready to join him in Heaven above.

34

UPSTAIRS

In Memory of Virginia Pauline Rowles

A life that shines like pure gold
Is a reflection of one's soul.
Having shared her talents and time
Helping other people by being kind.

The things we remember of her best
Have now ceased as she goes to rest.
Thanks to my family and friends
Who helped me live over threescore ten.

One who always expressed her cares,
Has now departed and gone upstairs
To enter her mansion in the sky
And to say to her family here, goodbye.

WHERE HE AWAITS

In Memory of B.W. Davis,
Sheriff of Spotsylvania

His guardian angel sounded the bell
With the message of death and all was well.
To depart from this world is not the end
Of one who has always been a friend.

Having lived this life for seventy years,
His departure brings sadness and tears;
But this will only be for a little while
As we remember him who always had a smile.

In his last days he suffered pain
But knowing Jesus, he had much to gain.
Everyone who knew him, knew his love
Which had been approved from Heaven above.

Trials and tests were a part of his life,
Shared with devoted family and loving wife.
Realizing whatever was sacrificed or lost
Has been replaced by the old rugged cross.

To give up a loved one brings much sorrow.
Our consolation is, we will see him tomorrow.
For one day we will join him were he awaits
As we leave this life and enter the pearly gates.

JUST GOODBYE

In Memory of Leon Acy (Buck) Bennett

He was truly a good man,
One who lived with a plan.
Helping many people without cost,
Willing to do this because he was boss.

Known by his laughter and his smile,
Strong in conviction but humble as a child.
He wanted everything done just right
Even though he had problems with his sight.

The time frame of his allotted life
Has been supported by a devoted wife.
His business was teamwork with his boys
But fishing and hunting were his greatest joys.

Separation has come after all these years
Leaving us with an emptiness and many tears.
Memories will always be our tie
He is not gone forever — just goodbye.

ETERNAL RHYTHM

In Memory of Mrs. Novella Hazzard Story

The death angel has called another one to glory,
This time the person's name was Mrs. Story.
She lived a life of many years
Knowing departure will bring sadness and tears.

Having been a loving, devoted mother and wife
To her husband and family all of her life.
To know her was to know a friend,
Willing to help anyone until the end.

Music was her great talent of love,
Having her heart in time with things above.
Now to join in with the choirs of Heaven
With the harps and music of eternal rhythm.

In her last days there was sickness and pain
But I never remember hearing her complain.
And now the time has come for eternal rest,
Believing Heaven is ours when we pass the test.

HEAVEN'S GATE

In Memory of Margaret Buckner

When in Heaven they open the book
And through the pages take a look,
The name of every person will be called
Who had been redeemed from the adamic fall.

Knowing Jesus who came to save
And has given life beyond the grave.
This salvation has been provided from above
For our Heavenly reservation by His love.

This life has offered suffering and pain
But death has released for Heaven's gain.
Where there are no tears, sickness, and sorrow
Life here in Christ is the beginning of tomorrow.

In Memory

VERNON SHIFFLETT

V ery active person in his work.
E ngaged also as a daily clerk.
R unning the business he enjoyed,
N ever forgetting he was employed.
O nly to give of his best,
N ight and day with little rest.

S miling throughout the day.
H appiness was the only way.
I nterested in the people he served.
F inding honesty would calm the nerve.
F aithful to his children and wife,
L eading them to know no strife.
E ncouraging others to consider life,
T ime is running out on this earth.
T aking Jesus as Savior is the Second Birth.

THE ANGEL'S CALL

In Memory of Sam Vanlandingham

Sam started cutting hair at the age of twenty
Would cut your hair even if there was no money.
He did his work with a great sense of joy
Cutting hair for anyone who came, man or boy.

Having only the one business for sixty years
When I was small he cut my hair and wiped my tears
He was always gentle, understanding and very kind
Never made a charge, just posted a sign.

Waiting customers would tell a hunting tale
His favorite sport was to hunt quail.
His gentle way to everyone was the same
Making no difference between age or name.

He loved his two daughters and his wife
And they were devoted to him during his life.
Everyone he met, he desired to make a friend
He was what he was and would not bend.

Now that he has heard the death angel's call
He left behind a message to be shared with us all.
Put your love in Christ and do your very best —
We'll see you in the morning, now I'm going to rest.

Written by:

G. Albert Brown, Jr.

March 4, 1989

41

ETERNAL REST

In Memory of Emmitt Dillard

I worked all day with joy
Trying to do my best.
I thought at times I was a boy,
But I knew I must take my rest.

When the day had closed its curtain
And the sun was set in the west
I examined my heart to be certain
For I knew the promise of eternal rest.

I came home at the close of the day
Knowing I had done my best.
I could honestly take my pay
Without any fear of a test.

When day has ended and night is come
We should inventory what we have given;
Because life on earth for some
Will be continued in Heaven.

READY FOR DEATH

In Memory of Alvin Winston Abbott

When he closed his eyes in sleep
He placed his soul in the Master's keep;
Knowing that everything was well with the soul,
Being prepared to cross over his ultimate goal.

He has suffered tremendously both night and day
Believing whatever happened, Christ was the way.
He was confident of a reserved place in Heaven
Which he knew that salvation in Christ had given.

He was a devoted membr of this church
Helping where he could in a soul-winning search;
Until one day he drew his last breath
To say, "Lord, I've done my best, I'm ready for death."

LIFE HAS NOT ENDED

In Memory of Lewin Randolph Brown, Jr.

At the end of life's day
When I closed my eyes in death
I heard a voice from Heaven say
As I drew my last breath.

Life has not come to an end
Because in Christ Jesus we live
Having crossed the threescore and ten
To enjoy all that Heaven will give.

As I enter into my eternal rest
I know there is no more sickness or sorrow
Through suffering and pain I gave my best
While waiting for this tomorrow.

For my family I did provide
Being devoted to my wife
Realizing time would help me decide
All the unanswered questions of this life.

So let me point you to a better way
As we seek the peace of our soul
Looking to Jesus with the Heavenly ray
Which illuminates for us the Calvary goal.

Friends

A TEN-YEAR TRIBUTE TO A FRIEND

M.E. Shelton

I think that we both would always agree
That our love is centered at Calvary,
Being conscious that our good health
Is the main source of anyone's wealth.

But to have and unselfishly share
Because people like you really care.
All your acts are centered in love
Knowing there is something greater above.

Whether we have health, wealth, or gold
It was Jesus Christ who redeemed our soul,
Because of every kindness on earth given
Faith in Christ has reserved a seat in Heaven.

The love you show for your loving wife
Is a true witness of a Christian life.
Whenever the Lord says this is the end
I want to be remembered as your pastor friend.

HEART OF GOLD

A Tribute to M.E. Shelton

If there ever was an honest soul
He is my friend with a heart of gold.
One who is concerned in the time of need
Willing to help with an unselfish deed.

He is a person devoted to his wife,
Living a good and dedicated life.
Whenever you see him he has a smile
Making me feel as if I am his child.

He has stored up many rewards above
With a life of demonstrating love.
To enter his home is like being under his wing
Willing to talk whenever the phone would ring.

He loves his church and his friends,
Knowing our integrity in Christ never ends.
Listening daily to know everything is well
This is my friend, who is known as **Shel**.

HAPPY BIRTHDAY — M.E. SHELTON

July 15, 1906 — 1988

(82 Years)

A man who has been special to me,
In the past and always will be.
Because of his concern and genuine love,
Will have special rewards from God above.

As his eyes are daily growing dim
And his aging days are a problem to him,
I want to help brighten his days as one
Who loves him as if I were his son.

BIRTHDAY POEM
BESSIE ELLIS SHELTON
MARCH 10, 1910

As one who is always happy and willing to say
My God has been so good to me everyday.
Now that she has reached seventy years and nine
Trusting something she has done for others will shine.

Much of her life is centered around church and friends
And her heart's desire is to be faithful until the end.
She has experienced many valleys and joys,
But always loved by her husband and boys.

If she had one request to leave with you,
Don't ever miss out on that which is true.
In all of earth's tangible silver and gold,
Nothing is as precious as Salvation of Soul.

CORDS OF LOVE

Written for my Christian friends, Milton and Evelyn Christy

One day as I went out walking
I heard two people as they were talking.
I listened attentively for a while
And then my face put on a big smile;

To hear them talking about the Word.
I took in everything that I heard.
It made a permanent lodging in my soul
Because the subject was as pure gold.

To know I had met a husband and wife
Who were not ashamed of eternal life.
They shared with me their testimony true,
Christ makes a difference for us and you.

With dedication and devotion they live.
To others in need, they are willing to give.
Using their talents and time for the King
With an expression of happiness they sing.

So when people like this become a friend,
They are what they are throughout the end;
Because true friends are very hard to find
Using only cords of love to unite and bind.

YOUR BEST

Written for Rev. Paige Young

of Ferry Farm Baptist Church

20th Anniversary Celebration — May 24, 1983

When one receives a divine call,
It means to give the Lord your all.
This I believe you have done,
Realizing there are crowns to be won.

Setting Heaven as an ultimate goal,
While recognizing the importance of a soul;
You prepared yourself His Gospel to preach
With a ministry for people everywhere to reach.

You have yielded Him your entire life,
Drawing on the help of a devoted wife,
Serving with an agape love,
Taking your orders from God above.

The people you have served have been just great,
Knowing together you will enter the Pearly Gate.
In these twenty years you have done your best,
Never to stop until the Lord says, rest.

A MAN OF DEDICATION

In Honor of Mr. Len Stevens on his retirement,
December 28, 1986

Len Stevens is a man of dedication,
Preaching the gospel without hesitation.
Being true to God's Holy Word
Without compromise wherever heard.

He has served his church a long term
While standing with his people firm.
They were blessed everytime he preached
And challenged them that others be reached.

As the music of the instruments would ring
He would start the people to sing
The good old hymns we always love
About salvation and Heaven's glory above.

We are confident he has done his best
Now comes the time for some rest,
And if you ever knew the preacher called Len,
You could mark it down, you knew a friend.

FRIENDSHIP

Written for Carl and Larry Silver

One day as I was in the business world
I met two businessmen, father and son.
We engaged in a conversation that was hurled
To realize a friendship between us has begun.

We talked about things of the old days
To discover that time changes the past,
Regardless of our methods or our ways
Knowing that memories will always last.

I knew the father when he was a boy
Because we are not far apart in years.
But the union of a father and a son brings joy
To know that success is dedication and tears.

These two men are honest and fair
As they go about their daily task,
Because they seek to let others share
In evey transaction that is cast.

I appreciate them more that words
Can find the description to express,
Because everything I have ever heard
Has been accredited to their success.

The world would be a better place to live
If people would learn to love one another.
It's not what we have, but what we give
Because true friendship can be like a mother.

When the truth has been earnestly sought
And the vision of our eyes made clear,
We will know that friendship has been taught
By the friend who is so close — He is near.

SEVEN-SEVENTEEN

Written for Roland Baker

At seven-seventeen Caroline Street
The owner of the business is waiting to greet.
You enter with your merchandise as the taker
To discuss your problems with Mr. Baker.

He will take a personal interest in you
As you share the need of your shoe.
The employees work with an ultimate goal
To give the best repairs for your sole.

He strives to give his customers the best
With long hours of work and little rest.
He repairs shoes of every kind,
Making them look like new with a shine.

He is concerned with everything you buy
Whether it be shoes, boots, or a lace to tie.
His friendliness will help you buy more
And cause you to always remember his store.

General

FATHER

It is always an experience very sad
When children have to give up their dad.
But when Christ is in the heart
It's not hard for him to depart.

Living on earth a life of love,
Spending eternity with friends above,
Leaves a testimony of a saved soul
Traveling the streets paved with gold.

No more tears, sickness, or sorrow,
Sealed in Christ for every tomorrow;
Waiting for my friends to follow me
So they too, in Heaven can be.

MOTHER

Our hearts are saddened to give up Mother
Because we know there is no other
Qualified to take her responsible place
As we search this God-given human race.

The pages of her life will always be a book
As we remember what she did and even her look.
She left with her family and friends Christian love
Knowing she had a prepared place above.

We know that we can see her again
Because Christ has atoned for all man's sin.
One day He is coming back again from Heaven
And then we will know all our blessings God has given.

SPRING IS LIFE

When the birds begin to sing,
We know it's time for Spring,
Because the weather will turn warm
And the cold has no more harm.

Spring is the year's most beautiful season
Bringing new life for its reason
As we see the leaves turn green
And breathe the air fresh and clean.

We know that winter has come and passed
And Spring has work for our task.
The ability to work increases with power
As the blessings of God supply the hour.

God's greatest blessing is the gift of His Son
For in Him eternal life is won.
Winter is like death with its cold,
But Spring is like life for the soul.

As seeds germinate in the earth
That they might give the plants birth,
We need the warmth of God's love
To know our hearts are planted above.

SNOW

When the ground is covered with a blanket of snow
It makes traveling difficult wherever you go.
The Lord said to the snow, Be there on earth,
And we should be grateful for all it's worth.

The snow is a filter to purify the air,
That the air we breathe might be clean everywhere.
The snow puts an abundant water supply into the ground
Which will help everybody in the country and in town.

The snow is beautiful while coming down
And with all its beauty, it has no sound.
The snow is measured sometimes by inches or by feet
Depending whether it's all snow or mixed with sleet.

The snow has a message in its beauty of white,
To let us know that every wrong can be made right
Regardless of who we are or what we know
If we will just trust Him who sends the snow.

BECAUSE OF YOU

Written for Howard Johnson Motel

When you come to the end of the day
And look for a good place to stay,
Choose Howard Johnson Motel for your rest
And you will discover you have the best.

Our food is good and the prices right
To add to the comfort of your night;
With service twenty-four hours around the clock,
Ready to serve you at every call and knock.

We, the staff, will greet you with a smile
Knowing your journey has been many a mile.
Tired and weary but happy to find
People who are always gracious and kind.

It's because of you that we are here
Wanting to be your friend and always near,
But when you leave remember this tip —
Pray for safety as you continue your trip.

(I served as Chaplain)

HAPPY TRAVELER

Written for Holiday Inn

For the traveler who is on his way
To find a place of rest
Will arrive at the close of the day
To discover Holiday Inn has the best.

The weary trip creates a frustrating mood
Which can be changed in the first hour,
With a well-balanced diet of good, cooked food,
And returning to my room for an evening shower.

We are here to please you in everything,
From the clerk to the boss —
Because we desire to serve you at every ring
For to mistreat you would be our loss.

To the business world let us convey
With guests like you our name is earned,
While we work hard to make your stay
So comfortable you will want to return.

Don't make this your last night
To enter through our swinging door;
As we seek to treat you right
That each time we might offer you more.

The Holiday Inn is not just a place
Where people come and go;
Our doors are opened to every race
That people everywhere might know —

We are always open to serve you,
Twenty-four hours around the clock,
The owners, management, staff, and chaplain, too
Will do anything for you while in our block.

(I served as Chaplain)

TODAY'S WISE MEN

Written for Fredericksburg Gideon Camp

The question has been asked
Where are the Wise Men of today?
Before the answer in haste is cast,
They have gathered on Saturday to pray.

The question has been sought,
Who are the Wise Men of today?
They are men after God's heart
Who are busy letting the Word say.

The question has been given,
Why do we need Wise Men today?
To carry out the mission of Heaven
That people might know the salvation way.

The question has been shared on earth,
When did the Wise Men get the message needed today?
It came with their visit of the Virgin Birth
As the eastern star cut off its ray.

The question of where, who, why, and when
May be discussed as they deliver the Word,
But the local camp of dedicated men
Will not stop until all have heard.

Now that we know their great task
And it's not to bring myrrh, frankincense, and gold
But in a quiet and unique mass
Give out their witness for the lost soul.

Beside everyone of these men
Stands his devoted wife
That the message of Christ continue to the end
Until all have heard the Way of eternal life.

Jesus, whom the Wise Men sought,
The Gideons of today share,
That people who desire to be taught
Can use the Bibles placed everywhere.

61

THE MESSAGE OF OUR SAVIOR

Christmas is a special season
When our hearts are full of joy;
But we should never forget the reason
Why God sent His Son as a boy.

He could have come as a full-grown man
Because there is nothing impossible with God.
The purpose was that He might stand
As God's representative upon this sod.

We do not understand the virgin birth
Because of the mystery it brings;
How He changed His abode from Heaven to earth
That from the manger to the cross salvation rings.

Let me tell you about His salvation plan
That only through God could be given.
It is free to every man
Because it began in Heaven.

He came to live among us
That we might know His way,
Because salvation through Christ is a must
If we hope to see that glorious day.

The cross brought the shedding of blood
And without it there is no remission.
Man had tried everything he could
But Calvary is God's commission.

YOUR PREACHER'S WIFE

There is one person in your church
That knows the preacher's life.
She weeps, smiles, and prays with him,
And that's your preacher's wife.

She knows his weakest point.
She knows his greatest power.
She gives him added strength
In his most needed hour.

She suffers with him in every hurt
As she listens to the agony of his soul.
With love and concern she speaks
Because she knows his goal.

My love grows greater every day
Because she is more than a wife;
While she gives me pulpit power
Every day of my preaching life.

TOGETHER FOR CHRIST

When he decided to answer the call to preach,
He was convinced it also meant to baptize and teach.
Through obedience, this he has very well done
Awaiting his crowns which have been won.

With the dedication of a searching soul
He has labored hard to reach his goal.
His service has been years of hard work
With sacrifice and commitment never to shirk.

His witness for Christ has been great,
Pointing many people to the Pearly Gates.
His gospel message has been "God is Love"
Which will turn our direction toward Him above.

He has given of himself that others may know
That all believers should witness as they go.
With the help of a loving and devoted wife
Together for Christ they have shared their life.

UNION OF TWO

I wanted a wife just like my daddy married,
That Mother's love might always be carried,
For the extension of the physical life
Which has been discovered in my loving wife.

This was true love at the very first sight,
To know the union of two which God will unite.
There are no words to explain true love
Especially when it comes down from above.

When God joins man and wife as one,
One half of life's program has been won.
With the attributes of honesty, faith, and trust
Because it's not a maybe — but a must!

Two women have made me what I am
With the dedication I received from both of them.
My mother and my wife will always be
Two special people very precious to me.

SEASON'S GREETINGS

Written by Mrs. Gladys Brown

T o say Merry Christmas
H ere's a greeting for you
E very good wish for the New Year, too.

A dore the Lord with zest
L et His day begin with the best.
B e of good cheer
E very good thing is wished for you here.
R emember always what happened on this day.
T hank the Lord for making a way.

B ehold, a Savior is born!
R ejoice in the hope that He will bring
O nly contentment in everything
W ith love adorn.
N ext glance at the letters beginning each line
S pelling who sent you this Christmas time rhyme.

MY HOME CHURCH

Written for the 100th Anniversary Homecoming
July 22, 1979, Cobham Park Baptist Church

In the year of Eighteen Eighty-Five
Some men in the Neck began to strive,
To find ways as they searched
To organize their own local church.

The only place of worship was so far
And no means of travel, not even a car.
Walking was good, though the distance was long
But our desire to worship spurred us on.

After three long, laborious years
With hard work, sweat, and tears
We chartered our own church in 1888,
And on our records we have placed the date.

Through a group of people in meditation,
Four years later was the dedication
Of a building that was given by God,
Located on a tract of Garland sod.

The building stood until the year of 1932
Having been built in the year of 1892.
Fourty years the building served the people.
By fire it was destroyed, even the steeple.

Another building was built by raising funds,
Ones who could not give, labor was done.
This building still stands with its additions
To be disassembled having served it's mission.

The building has been a source of light
As a monument guiding people in the right,
With evangelism being the outreach
And nothing but the Bible to preach.

MY HOME CHURCH

(continued)

Many have been turned from the wrong
And receiving new life with a song;
Sharing with others the gospel story
How Jesus came to earth from Heaven's glory.

The dedicated members of today
Have worked long and hard in their way,
Having accomplished much by the task
Realizing only what is done for Christ will last.

One day the angel will give the trumpet call
To open graves and take us all
Who are recorded in the Lamb's book up there
That Heaven will be ours as we meet Him in the air.

DEACON

A deacon has been set apart
With strong convictions in his heart.
Having been elected to the call
To be a servant in the church to all.

Realizing your obedience to the task.
Never guilty of wearing a disguising mask.
Supporting the total program of the church.
Concerned for the lost with a daily search.

In an attitude of prayer as you serve,
Always on guard for Satan's curve.
Knowing your position is not the preacher,
But aiding your pastor as a reacher.

Giving an account for every deed.
Believing God will supply your need.
Striving always to do your best
Before you lay down your position in rest.

NOT WHAT I GET BUT WHAT I GIVE

Not what I get,
　　But what I give,
This is the gauge,
　　By which I live.

Not merely joys,
　　That come my way;
But the help,
　　I give to those astray.

Not the rewards
　　Of money and fame;
But the loads,
　　I lift in Jesus' name.

This be the pay,
　　At the end of the day;
Not what I keep, but
　　What I give away.

Special Thoughts

PRAYER FOR HOUSE OF DELEGATES
January 22, 1985

Almighty God, Creator of the universe, we enter into Your Holy Presence recognizing the importance of prayer, asking for Your Divine guidance to rest upon each member of the House of Delegates and that every decision may reflect an attitude of wisdom and courage while they are in session.

Being grateful for our democracy, let them always remember our supreme governing power from above, knowing that God's banner over us is love, and that each member of this legislative body be reminded that every action should always be sought in His will, with a concern for the personal needs of their constituents. Through commitment and loyalty may they continue to serve our beloved Commonwealth with a humble spirit and a heart of understanding.

Let us express our gratitude to God, the Governor, and each member of the House of Delegates for all past accomplishments and trusting the future will be fruitful for the good of everyone, we pray in the name of Jesus Christ.

Amen.

(A Great Honor for Rev. G. Albert Brown, Jr.)

PRAYER FOR STATE SENATE
January 30, 1985

Almighty God, in Whom we put our trust, let us thank You for the privilege of prayer, being conscious at all times of Your Holy Presence.

We would ask that a demonstration of Your Divine power and continued blessings abide upon each member of this legislative body while they are in session, that each decision and action would reflect an attitude of wisdom and courage as they seek to meet the needs of their constituents.

Being grateful for our democracy, may each of the senators be united in purpose and willing to submit to the higher power of God for direction and instruction as they seek to plan and provide for our great Commonwealth.

As we look upon the past accomplishments, may they be used as examples to better prepare for the future with love and concern for all mankind, realizing that together we stand, divided we fall.

Thanking God for our senators and their dedication, help them to never forget that our nation was founded on the principles of God's Word and to Him we will be accountable.

This is our prayer in the name of Jesus Christ, our Savior and Lord.

Amen.

(A Great Honor for Rev. G. Albert Brown, Jr.)

THE HEAVENLY GROCERY STORE

— Anonymous —

I was walking down life's highway a long time ago
And one day I saw a sign that read, Heaven's Grocery Store.
As I got a little closer and the door came open wide,
I came to myself and I was standing inside.
I saw a host of angels who were standing everywhere,
One handed me a basket and said, Child, shop with care.
Everything a Christian needed was in that grocery store
And all you couldn't carry, you could come back for more.
First I got some patience, love was in the same row;
Further down was understanding, you need that everywhere
    you go.
I got a box or two of wisdom, a bag or two of faith,
And I just couldn't miss the Holy Ghost, for it was all over
    the place.
I stopped to get some strength and courage to help me run
    the race,
By then my basket was getting full, but I remembered I needed
    some grace.
I didn't forget salvation, for salvation was always free,
So I tried to get enough of that to save both you and me.
Then I started to the counter to pay my grocery bill
For I thought I had everything to do my Master's will.
As I went up the aisle I saw prayer, I just had to put that in,
For I knew when I stepped outside, I would run right into sin.
Peace and joy were plentiful, they were there on the last shelf.
Songs and praises were hanging near, so I just helped myself.
Then I said to an angel, Now how much do I owe?
He just smiled and said, Take them everywhere you go.
Again I smiled at him and said, Really, how much do I owe?
He smiled and said, My Child, **Jesus paid your bill**
    a long time ago.

THE EVOLUTIONISTS COULD BE RIGHT

— Anonymous —

Darwin Theory: A species of plants and animals developed from earlier forms by hereditary transmission of slight variation in successive generations and that the forms which survive are those best adapted to the enviroment.

Maybe people did descend from lower animals
Because church folks are often seen as:

*

Stubborn as mules about church work.
Sly as a fox in their business deals.
Busy as bees in spreading the latest gossip.
Blind as a bat to the world's need.
Quiet as a mouse in spreading the Gospel.
Eyes like a hawk to see the mote in their brother's eye.
Eager as a beaver about a bazaar or a barbeque.
Lazy as a dog about prayer meetings.
Mean as a snake when things don't go their way.
Gentle as a lamb when they need the Pastor's aid.
Noisy as a crow for the church to advance.
Slow as snails in visiting the unchurched.
Night owls on Saturday night.
Bed bugs on Sunday morning.
Slippery as eels on Sunday night.
Scarce as hen's teeth on Wednesday night.

*

Dr. Brown observes: Even a turtle wouldn't get anywhere unless he stuck his neck out.

Songs

VICTORY IN JESUS

Words and Music by E.M. Bartlett

Theme Song
of the Fredericksburg Bible Institute

I heard an old, old story, how a Savior came from glory,
How He gave His life on Calvary to save a wretch like me:
I heard about His groaning, of His precious blood's atoning,
Then I repented of my sins and won the victory.

I heard about His healing, of His cleansing power revealing,
How He made the lame to walk again and caused the blind to see;
And then I cried, dear Jesus, come and heal my broken spirit,
And somehow Jesus came and brought to me the victory.

I heard about a mansion He has built for me in glory,
And I heard about the streets of gold beyond the crystal sea;
About the angels singing, and the old redemption story,
And some sweet day I'll sing up there the song of victory.

CHORUS:

O, victory in Jesus, my Savior, forever
He sought me and bought me with His redeeming blood;
He loved me ere I knew Him, and all my love is due Him,
He plunged me to victory, beneath the cleansing flood.

I'LL SEE YOU IN THE RAPTURE

Words and Music by Charles B. Feltner

(Used In Radio Ministry — WORD OF TRUTH)

If we never meet again on this earth, my precious friend,
If, to God, we have been true and we've lived above all sin;
Then, for us, there'll be a greeting, for there's gonna be a meeting,
I'll see you in the rapture some sweet day.

To my loved ones let me say that there'll surely come a day
When the Lord will come again and He'll take His bride away;
So get ready now to meet Him, and with hallelujahs greet Him,
I'll see you in the rapture some sweet day.

CHORUS:

I'll see you in the rapture, see you in the rapture,
See you at that meeting in the air;
There, with our blessed Savior, we'll live and reign forever,
I'll see you in the rapture some sweet day.

I KNOW HIM

When the waves of temptation come,
I know Him, who calms the sea.
When unanswered questions arise,
I know Him, to whom I can go on bended knee.

When the journey of life is hard,
I know Him, who never leaves me alone.
When the foundation seems to be weak,
I know Him, who is my cornerstone.

When it seems there is no one to turn to,
I know Him, who is present every hour.
When it seems I can't go any further,
I know Him, the source of my power.

CHORUS:

His name is Jesus,
The sweetest name I know.
Always ready to help me,
Regardless of where I go.

WAITING ON THE LORD
Based on Isaiah 40:31

The people who are willing to wait
Upon the Lord who is ready to give;
Will never appear before Him late
Because of His mercy while we live.

They shall mount up with wings
Like the eagle from the blue,
With a soaring voice to sing
As our strength He will renew.

This strength will give us added power
To run the race of Christian love,
Being never weary for the great hour
When we can claim His promises from above.

To wait on God will be a spiritual walk
Without the danger that one might faint;
Realizing to wait on Him is to talk
That we might be His blessed saint.

CHORUS:

Waiting on the Lord
That His message may be heard.
Waiting on the Lord
For the promise of His word.

Waiting on the Lord
His blessings have we sought,
Waiting on the Lord
For with His blood He bought.

81

THE POWER OF GOD'S LIGHT

When man was created
He lost his sense of sight,
Sin began to dominate
And turned off all the light.

But the search through agony
Of the power from above
Was turned on at Calvary
With Jesus and His love.

This power will control
And give sense of glow
Every believing, living soul
With a spirit-filled halo.

All the darkness of the past
Will be put out of the way
With the light that will last
Throughout that eternal day.

CHORUS:

Give me that light
Give me that light
The only source of light
That will guide me in the right.

Give me that light
Give me that light
The only source of light
That will guide me day and night.

GOD'S GRACE FOR EVERY RACE

When God created the human race
He at the same time provided grace,
God knew that man would fall
So His grace was for whosoever would call.

Man fell into a state of sin,
Knowing not that it would begin
But God looked down from Heaven
With His mercy to be given.

He saw the human race was lost
So He provided His grace at the cross.
Jesus left the ivory palaces of glory
That the whole world might know His story.

Dying condemned, but an innocent man
Once for all breaking the sin band.
That we might all be set free
And reconciled to Heaven with Thee.

Now salvation has come by His love
Because it came to us from above.
It's not the color of one's skin
But God's grace is salvation from sin.

Your sin though scarlet it may be
Can be made white as snow at Calvary.
Christ's mission was to seek and save
That we might have eternal life beyond the grave.

CHORUS:

God's grace is sufficient for all mankind
God's grace is sufficient at any time
God's grace is sufficient for all who taste
God's grace is His love for every race.

SECOND BIRTH

Jesus came down from Heaven above
That we might learn of God's love;
Through giving to us the Father's Plan
That salvation would be available to every man.

Jesus lived in a demonstration of grace
That all may see in Him the Father's face,
Jesus gave up His life in death on the cross
Finishing His work while dying for the loss.

Jesus arose from the grave to live
That through His life, assurance to give;
Eternal security to every redeemed soul
That union with Him is our ultimate goal.

Jesus is coming one day back to earth
For all who have experienced second birth,
And let the brightness of that sacred hour
Will let us know the fullness of His power.

CHORUS:

Jesus...Jesus...Jesus...Who came to the earth.
Jesus...Jesus...Jesus...Who gave the Second Birth.

Notes

and

Quotes

FAVORITE SAYINGS

- Behind every successful man stands a devoted wife and a surprised mother-in-law.

- If someone sets out to destroy you, live so no other person will believe it.

- You cannot talk the talk unless you walk the walk.

- If a person gets burned, he should stay away from the fire.

- Always tell the truth and you will never have to change your story.

- The greatest investment you will ever make is that which pays off for Christ.

- The more you give away, the more will be given to you.

- *Wheelbarrow Christians:*
    He has to be pushed,
    He runs on one wheel,
    He is easily upset.

- *Inkblotter Christians:*
    He picks up everything he touches,
    But he gets it all backwards.

- If you are born again
  You are a saint.
  If you are not born again
  You are a ain't.

- A Chameleon Christian is one that can change to any situation — right or wrong.

FAVORITE SAYINGS

- If you are too big to take criticism,
  You are too small to be praised.

- You may talk about me all you please,
  If you do your talking on your knees.

- It is not whether you win or lose,
  But it is how you play the game.

- The only time rock and roll is all right
  Is if your feet are on the rock
  And your name is on the roll.

- Laughter is better than medicine.

- Smiles is the longest word in the English language...
  A mile between two s's.

- The family that prays together
  Is the family that stays together.

- "The only way someone can kick you from behind is when you are
  in the front."

- "Every time my eyes are closed — I'm not asleep."

- "If you haven't suffered test or trial, it is a good indication you
  haven't done anything."

- It takes diplomacy to get a diploma.

- Don't give till it hurts;
  Give a little more
  Give till it feels good.

FAVORITE SAYINGS

- Grace is what God has given that we do not deserve.
  Mercy is what God has withheld from us that we do deserve.

- A knowledge of the Bible without a college education is far greater than a college education without a knowledge of the Bible.

- A quitter never wins
  And a winner never quits.

- A hypocrite is one who is lost
  A backslider is one who is saved but acts like a hypocrite.

FAVORITE QUOTES

- "I am profitably engaged in reading the Bible. Take all of this book upon reason that you can, and the balance by faith, and you will live and die a better man."

  —Abraham Lincoln

- "I have a very simple thing to ask of you. I ask every man and woman in this audience that from this day on they will realize that part of the destiny of America lies in their daily perusal of this great Book."

  —Woodrow Wilson

- "Believe me, Sir, never a night goes by, be I ever so tired, but I read the Word of God before I go to bed."

  — Douglas MacArthur

- "To read the Bible is to take a trip to a fair land, where the spirit is strengthened and faith renewed."

  —Dwight D. Eisenhower

- "It is impossible to rightly govern the world without God and the Bible."

  — George Washington

I want to personally thank all the contributors and those who helped me assemble this book, especially Mrs. Donna Schwertfeger, the typist.

"Comfort one another with these words."
I Thessalonians 4:18